D0948705

EXPLORING CAREERS IN TV AND FILM

Makeup and Styling in TV and Film

Jeri Freedman

Cavendish Square
New York

Published in 2019 by Cavendish Square Publishing, LLC
243 5th Avenue, Suite 136, New York, NY 10016

Library of Congress Cataloging-in-Publication Data

Names: Freedman, Jeri.
Title: Makeup and styling in TV and film / Jeri Freedman.
Description: New York : Cavendish Square, 2019. | Series: Exploring careers in TV and film | Includes glossary and index.
Identifiers: ISBN 9781502641250 (pbk.) | ISBN 9781502641267 (library bound) | ISBN 9781502641274 (ebook)
Subjects: LCSH: Television makeup--Juvenile literature. | Film makeup--Juvenile literature. | Film makeup--Vocational guidance--Juvenile literature. | Hairdressing--Vocational guidance--Juvenile literature. | Costume--Vocational guidance--Juvenile literature.
Classification: LCC PN2068.F64 2019 | DDC 792'.027--dc23

Editorial Director: David McNamara
Editor: Kristen Susienka
Copy Editor: Rebecca Rohan
Associate Art Director: Alan Sliwinski
Designer: Christina Shults
Production Coordinator: Karol Szymczuk
Photo Research: J8 Media

The photographs in this book are used by permission and through the courtesy of: Cover Alexander Kirch/Shutterstock.com; p. 4 Jeff Spicer/Getty Images; p. 8 Thomas Trutschel/Photothek/Getty Images; p. 10 ©Universal/courtesy Everett Collection; p. 16 Narinder Nanu/AFP/Getty Images; p. 22 Murray Close/Moviepix/Getty Images; p. 27 Barcroft Media/Getty Images; p. 28 Rodin Eckenroth/WireImage/Getty Images; p. 31 Makeartnotwar/Shutterstock.com; p. 33 Nejron Photo/Shutterstock.com; p. 34 Michael Tullberg/Getty Images; p. 37 AFP/Getty Images; p. 38 Putu Sayoga/Getty Images; p. 39 Fairfax Media/Getty Images; p. 41 Joan Vicent Cantó Roig/E+/Getty Images; p. 43 ©Walt Disney Studios Motion Pictures/Courtesy Everett Collection; p. 44 Nicole Deshayes/AFP/Getty Images; p. 47 Rick Loomis/Los Angeles Times/Getty Images; p. 52 Catalin Petolea/Shutterstock.com; p. 54 Creatista/Shutterstock.com; p. 58 Frederick Florin/AFP/Getty Images; p. 65 imageBROKER/Alamy Stock Photo; p. 72 Visual China Group/Getty Images; p. 75 Chaoss/Shutterstock.com; p. 81 GaudiLab/Shutterstock.com; p. 84 Anthony Harvey/WireImage/Getty Images; p. 85 J. Stone/Shutterstock.com.

Printed in the United States of America

CONTENTS

A hairstylist fixes an actor's hair prior to an appearance on television.

CHAPTER ONE

Working in the Industry

Makeup artists and stylists play an integral role in creating the characters portrayed by actors on television and in films. In the twenty-first century, increases in the number of companies producing film and television shows and new avenues of delivery have created more opportunities for makeup artists and hair stylists than ever before.

By the Numbers

According to the statistics website Statista, the global film industry revenue was estimated to be $38 billion in 2016 and projected to increase to almost $50 billion in 2020. With about 5,800 cinemas, the United States is the third-largest market for films, based on ticket sales. Only China and India have larger film markets. Thirteen percent of Americans see movies in a cinema once a month and 7 percent go out to see movies several times a month, whereas 52 percent of American adults prefer watching movies at home, and the rest go to a cinema less than once a month.

According to the Motion Picture Association of America (MPAA), 718 movies were released in North

America in 2016. Among the largest film studios are Walt Disney (parent company of Buena Vista, Pixar, Marvel Studios, and Lucasfilm), Time Warner (parent company of Warner Brothers), 21st Century Fox, NBC Universal, and Viacom (parent company of Paramount). These Hollywood studios concentrate mostly on big-budget blockbusters, such as *Wonder Woman* and *Star Wars*, which offer huge ticket sales, tie-in merchandising opportunities, and the promise of sequels. The Hollywood studios are not the only source of films, however. Alternate media companies such as Netflix, known for its original streaming TV programming, are also venturing into moviemaking.

Independent films are, by definition, made with private financing, as opposed to studio funding. Typically, independent films take more risks with style and content than studio films. They rarely cost more than $20 million to make, and many cost less than $10 million. According to the MPAA, independent films accounted for 579 of the 718 films released in 2016. This is important for those wishing to break into film production as makeup artists or stylists. In order to work on a studio film, a person must be a member of the makeup or stylists union, but to become a union member, an individual must have experience doing makeup or styling on a film. One way to gain this experience is to work on independent, nonunion films.

The line between strictly independent films and Hollywood movies is being blurred. Some major studios have instituted divisions that finance and/or distribute independent films. These films don't bring in the amount of revenue that big-budget Hollywood blockbusters do. However, they capture a percentage of the audience that the studios want to tap into, they provide revenue from on-demand licensing and DVD sales, and they often garner awards, which bring prestige to the studio. An example of such a studio branch is Fox Searchlight Pictures, which has provided support for such films as *Slumdog Millionaire*, *Birdman*, and *The Shape of Water*, which won the Academy Award for Best Picture in 2018.

TV is the medium with the largest reach. According to Statista, 90 percent of the US population watches TV, and on average most people watch four hours of TV per day. The advent of streaming services such as Netflix, Amazon Video, and Hulu; network offerings such as HBO Now and CBS All Access; and on-demand services offered by cable and satellite TV providers has contributed to this trend. In 2017, 29 percent of US households had a smart TV, which can access streaming and on-demand services. The global online television industry is growing rapidly. In 2017, there were approximately 124 million subscription video-on-demand users in the United States. Statista indicates that this number is expected to grow to 160 million by 2022, and 32 percent of global viewers are expected to subscribe to such services.

An increasing number of young affluent viewers watch TV over the internet, rather than subscribing to traditional cable or satellite television providers. Those in this demographic tend to be heavy users of

Netflix is the largest television streaming service, providing popular TV shows and movies as well as original content.

mobile technology, especially smartphones, and they like the convenience of being able to watch where and when they choose. There were 32.5 million viewers in 2016 who had never subscribed to traditional television services, and Statista forecasts that this number will grow to 41 million by 2021.

Not everyone is switching from traditional TV, however. In the 2017/2018 season, the number of households subscribing to traditional TV grew slightly, reversing a downward trend in previous seasons. One possible reason for this is that more millennials are moving out of family homes to start their own households.

All these trends are good news for aspiring makeup artists and stylists. The need to constantly provide new content to binge-watching audiences, along with the competition among the major providers, has led to more TV shows being produced than ever before. More production means more demand for makeup artists and stylists. A large subset of the on-demand television industry is videos made for delivery over the internet by services such as YouTube and a wide range of specialty websites. Unlike other forms of entertainment, these videos can be produced by anyone who understands how to shoot video and upload it, including high-school students. This type of venue provides an excellent opportunity to work on one's makeup and styling skills while still in school.

Being a Makeup Artist or Stylist

Each production has its own requirements for makeup and hairstyling, but they usually fall into one of three categories: enhancing beauty, reducing flaws, or altering a character's appearance— sometimes radically.

Makeup artists use cosmetics, prostheses, and other tools to turn an actor into the director's conception of a character in a film or TV show. Stylists arrange, color, and cut hair for the same purpose. Special-effects makeup artists use not only cosmetics and prostheses but also mechanical and electronic components, which might incorporate light, sound, or motion effects. They create fantasy, alien, or horror characters, as well as human characters whose appearance has

Historical dramas, such as the movie *Elizabeth*, require makeup artists and stylists to capture the look of people of that time.

been drastically changed—for example, the survivor of a fire with third-degree burns or the victim of a werewolf attack with horrible wounds.

Makeup artists and stylists work on film and television productions, in theme parks, and for private clients such as fashion designers or celebrities. A makeup artist or stylist's work can range from making an actress look more attractive (beauty makeup) to making a young actor age over the course of a production (age makeup) to creating an alien life form or horrible monster (special-effects makeup). Job growth for makeup artists is expected to be 12 percent annually from 2016 to 2026, which is faster than average. The US Bureau of Labor Statistics (BLS) states that the field of cosmetology—which includes hairdressers and hair stylists as well as makeup artists—is expected to see average job growth of 13 percent from 2016 to 2026, although this number is not limited to those working in the film and television industry.

Succeeding in Makeup and Styling

There are a number of qualities that will help a person succeed in makeup and styling. Some of these skills are technical, but many are personal qualities and interpersonal skills. For makeup artists, technical skills include the ability to sculpt in clay, which also requires an understanding of anatomy. Makeup artists often create masklike features to change an actor's facial appearance, so sculpting is a key skill. Even when they are creating makeup for nonhuman characters, having knowledge of anatomy allows them to understand how muscles, bones, and joints work. In addition to sculpting, color and painting skills are necessary. These professionals are called makeup *artists* for a reason. It's not necessary to be Rembrandt, but one has to know how to apply colors effectively to masks, appliances, and actors' skin with a brush and airbrush. Knowing how colors work and blend together is called color theory. It's important for people in the makeup industry to know and understand this concept. Those who are interested in special-effects makeup also need to learn basic electric and electronic principles so they can design and wire special effects. Stylists will need to learn hairdressing and cutting skills.

Both makeup and hairstyling make use of particular materials and tools with which the professional needs to be familiar. Increasingly, special-effects makeup artists must learn graphics and computer-modeling software. Special-effects makeup might require a combination of physical and computer-generated effects. Even if the makeup artist is only responsible for the physical aspects of the makeup and related props, he or she must be able to collaborate with the technician generating the digital effect. An understanding of the general principles of such programs helps with this process.

Makeup is both an art and a science. In addition to color theory, the professional needs to understand hygiene, to keep their tools sanitary; anatomy and bone structure, for contouring and special-effects design;

and chemistry, to understand which chemicals can safely be combined and how to work with molding compounds, glues, and solvents. A person can begin to learn the necessary technical skills while in high school. Students can lay the foundation for learning these subjects by taking high school math, biology, chemistry, physics, and art classes. In most cases, they will take additional courses in makeup and styling after high school.

High school is the perfect time to enhance personal qualities and interpersonal skills as well. It is often a stressful and competitive time—the perfect training ground for a career in film or television production, both of which are often high-pressure and competitive environments. The following are some skills that help a person succeed in these fields:

- **Listening skills.** Film or television makeup or styling professionals must have strong listening skills so that they are certain to understand and correctly follow directors' instructions.

- **Paying attention.** Production artists must be attentive to detail. Small details make a significant difference to the effectiveness and believability of their creations. Attention to detail is also critical for eliminating flaws that will be visible to the camera, which often produces a very close view of characters.

- **Observing.** Good observational skills are important as well. Noticing the details of how real people normally look is the basis for creating new and different characters.

- **Cooperation.** Makeup and styling professionals must get along well with people. When elements don't work as expected, when constant changes have to be made, and when things go wrong and have to be fixed, the ability to maintain an even temper and remain positive and polite is key to getting along with others on the job.

- **Solving problems.** Production artists must be able to tolerate frustration and solve problems— not only when they have lots of time, but also on the fly and with the materials on hand. Changes are a constant in film and TV production, so the ability to be flexible, to adapt one's work, and to improvise will make one more successful and gain the respect of coworkers.

- **Different schedules.** Film and TV shows have tight schedules, and shooting often takes place outside of normal working hours. Therefore, makeup and styling professionals must be willing to work early in the morning or late at night, and to work long hours to meet deadlines.

- **Organization.** Good organizational skills are also very important. Makeup and styling professionals need to prepare many actors for a single shoot and may need to juggle multiple projects. Therefore, they must be able to identify priorities, arrange tasks in an order that will get them all done when required, and manage their time well.

Often, makeup and styling professionals will work as part of a team—this is almost a certainty for those just starting out. They must be able to communicate well with other members of the team, make positive contributions, and be willing to help others when necessary.

One skill that can't be taught but can be practiced is imagination. The element that sets great makeup artists and stylists apart is the ability to imagine unique, striking, or beautiful versions of the makeup and styles required for film and television productions. Being a makeup artist or stylist isn't easy, but it is interesting and creative, and it offers the great satisfaction of seeing one's work onscreen.

Cast and crew members start shooting a scene of the Punjabi movie *Aasra*.

CHAPTER TWO

The Team

Creating a film or TV show is a group effort and requires a large team of creative and production professionals. Because of the collaborative nature of filmmaking, it is important for makeup artists and stylists to be able to work well with the other members of the team, even under stressful conditions. The relationships between artists and other team members can determine whether or not they succeed. If these individuals work for a company hired by the studio, good relationships can mean that the company will be invited to work on future projects. On the other hand, bad relationships or experiences can ruin a career.

The Creative Team

Every day the makeup and styling departments interact with major professionals also working on the film or TV project. The professionals in these roles function as department heads. They hire the staff who perform the tasks in their area. They might supervise studio staff, hire freelancers, or subcontract other companies, such as those who create props or special effects.

Producer

The producer is essentially the chief executive officer (CEO) of a film or TV series. He or she locates or approves the property to be made into films. This might be an original script or series concept, a novel, or a work from another medium that he or she believes could be effectively adapted.

After finding a script or concept, the producer obtains financing for the project. In the case of a studio project, this means pitching the idea to studio executives to get approval and funds for the project. In the case of independent films or videos, it means getting individuals or companies to invest in the project.

After funds are obtained, the producer creates the budget and makes sure that costs stay within the amount of funding available. The producer is not just responsible for the business aspects of a project, however. He or she will generally hire the director and writer(s).

Director

The director exercises artistic control over a film or television show. He or she hires the head of the production teams and actors, oversees the design of the project, and makes the creative decisions as to how the movie or TV show is filmed. After filming, the director works with the film editor to create the final version of the film.

Because the director creates the overall vision for the production, his or her decisions influence the makeup and styling used for the actors. The heads of these departments receive information from the director on the look and/or special effects he or she wants. They then submit designs for approval. Once approval is received, the film and styling departments must create the makeup and hairstyles selected.

Cinematographer

The cinematographer, or director of photography (DP), is the head of the camera and lighting departments. He or she shoots or supervises the actual shooting of the film. The cinematographer works closely with the director, making the decisions that create the look and feel of the film or TV show, through the design of lighting and camera shots and angles. These decisions will influence the requirements for makeup and styling in terms of both visibility and atmosphere.

The Production Team

The production team is an essential part of any TV program or film. The makeup artist and stylist work closely with the entire team to ensure each character comes to life in the way the director and screenplay dictate.

Production Manager

Production managers oversee the business aspects of the production departments. They do not make creative decisions, but they control and monitor the production budget and approve expenditures. They also book resources, equipment, subcontractors, and locations for shooting.

Production Designer/Art Director

The production designer's job is to create the film's overall "look." He or she works closely with the director. The production designer is responsible for the sets, costumes, makeup, hairstyling, props, and other physical aspects of a film. The term "production designer" is sometimes used interchangeably with "art director," and in smaller projects they are often one and the same. In large projects, the production designer's second-in-command is designated as art director. In this case, the art director works with the production department heads to make sure their designs correspond to the concepts of the production designer and that work proceeds as needed.

Set Designer

The set designer creates the concept for the sets for a film or TV show, including the interiors and exteriors and their incidental elements, such as furnishings and props. The set department constructs the sets according to the design, and the set dresser collects appropriate props. The costumes, makeup, and sets must all work together to create the appropriate atmosphere for the project.

The Costume Designer

The costume designer is responsible for creating all the clothing worn by the cast of a film or TV show. He or she chooses the fabrics and colors worn by characters and designs their outfits. Their designs, along with makeup and hairstyling, capture the mood, status, and other personal aspects of the roles. The costume designer also designs or acquires accessories for the characters.

The Makeup and Hair Team

Makeup artists and stylists must have a thorough understanding of film and TV production as well as the techniques of makeup and hair design and creation. They need to integrate their work with that of other creative production departments to create an appropriate look and feel for a character. They need knowledge of, or the willingness to research, a variety of cultures and historical periods. They must create makeup that captures the story of the project and that reflects characters' attitudes, culture, age, status, and physical condition. And different types of makeup and variations in hair will likely need to be applied to actors over the course of the film or TV show.

The head of the makeup and hair department is the key makeup artist. However, very large projects may have a department head and a key makeup artist. The former handles the business of running the department, such as budgeting and hiring, and the latter manages the creative aspects. Usually, the key makeup artist designs the makeup that will be worn by all the actors in the film or TV show, and the makeup artists apply the makeup to individual actors. In some cases, they apply natural-looking makeup that doesn't change the actors' appearance, but merely keeps them looking neat and not pale or shiny on television. In other cases, they apply makeup that enhances the actors' attractiveness or covers flaws. Special-effects

For his role as Beast in *X-Men: First Class*, actor Nicholas Hoult required makeup that was both mutant-like and natural looking.

makeup artists specialize in radically changing actors' appearance. They might make them look like aliens or demons, or survivors of a cataclysmic disaster. They also create more limited effects such as wounds. Sometimes special-effects makeup artists are called on to create parts of the makeup that produce sound or motion as well.

Makeup assistants help apply makeup under the direction of a makeup artist. They are necessary when working on a project in which a large number of actors have to be made up for a film scene or TV show episode.

Hair stylists create the hairdos worn by actors. As with makeup artists, their work ranges from making actors look attractive to creating elaborate historically accurate hairdos—or even unusual alien-looking hairpieces. Hair assistants help hair stylists prepare and style actors.

Working with the Team

A makeup artist or stylist in the entertainment industry has a responsibility for ensuring the success of both the makeup and hair team and the larger team that is producing the project. Makeup artists and stylists must have trust in other team members and make sure those team members can count on them. Accomplishing this means developing good time management and planning skills. On one hand, this means being willing to speak up when they feel that an approach they have conceived would enhance

THE PERKS OF A MAKEUP OR STYLIST CAREER

There are a variety of perks to being a makeup artist or stylist. Makeup artists and stylists for TV and film get to experiment with looks, tools, and materials. Fresh makeup tools and techniques are constantly being developed; so are new film and television technologies. Thus, there is always something new on the horizon.

Film and television communities offer the opportunity to be a part of a close-knit group and develop friendships with others who share one's interests. Makeup artists and stylists also meet other interesting people, both celebrities and artists known for their behind-the-scenes accomplishments. More importantly, they have the opportunity to make celebrities and others look good. The work is challenging—an artist and stylist can try different types of real-world and otherworldly looks on actors who have different skin, hair, and body types. If they reach the point at which celebrities specifically request them to do their makeup or hair, this can provide both professional and personal satisfaction.

Makeup artists and stylists have access to the backlot of the studio(s) where they work, giving them a firsthand view of how movies and television shows are made. There is the satisfaction of seeing one's work on the big or small screen and one's name in the credits. At some point in their career, an artist or stylist is likely to be asked to travel to other cities—or even other countries—to work on projects. This gives them the chance to see interesting locations at the studio's expense.

Early in a makeup artist or stylist's career, they'll likely work for a studio or special-effects makeup company on a regular, full- or part-time basis, or they'll accept every job that comes their way to make a living. As they advance, however, they can choose to work as a freelancer if they want, which allows them to pick the projects they want to work on and when they want to work.

Although many people are not going to make a lot of money in their first entry-level job, the makeup field pays well, and as a person gains recognition, he or she can earn a significant amount.

Further, makeup work provides great flexibility. If at some point he or she decides they prefer a different environment, they can apply their skills to other areas that employ makeup artists, such as fashion photography, advertising, or public relations, or they can even open their own salon.

As a person progresses in their makeup or styling career, he or she will have the opportunity to gain professional recognition. In addition to possibly winning awards, he or she could be asked to write online or print articles, create a blog, or appear on a segment of a TV show.

the success of the makeup or hair. On the other hand, it may mean putting aside their own preferences to comply with the design decisions once they have been made.

Makeup artists and stylists must make sure that even the small details of their work are as perfect as possible. Even tiny flaws can ruin the realism of makeup as it is being shot. Professionals must be willing to do boring repetitive tasks efficiently, especially when starting out, not just interesting creative work. Each team member must constantly communicate what he or she is doing and stay aware of what others are working on as well so that the work is consistent and complementary. Doing this helps the project stay on schedule. At the same time, makeup artists and stylists must be able to complete their share of the work independently.

Team members must be willing to help each other. They need to pitch in when a task needs extra hands, and they need to be able to give constructive advice without demeaning other team members or sounding negative. It's important to keep a sense of humor and be positive about the work. Creating a good atmosphere in which to work helps mitigate the stress of working long hours under time constraints. It builds a sense of support and friendship among team members.

Those who want to succeed in doing movie or television makeup or hairstyling must realize that the vision for the work is the result of collaboration, and that they may need to compromise to achieve an optimal result. Makeup artists and stylists must be flexible in terms of work, hours, concepts, and changes

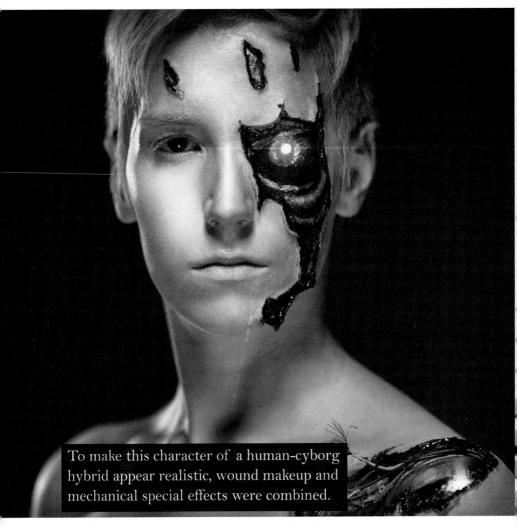

To make this character of a human-cyborg hybrid appear realistic, wound makeup and mechanical special effects were combined.

resulting from practical problems and alterations in the script. A team that works together well can produce a result everyone is proud of.

A makeup artist touches up an actress's makeup between scenes to ensure her face remains perfect.

CHAPTER THREE

Working on a Production

Makeup artists and stylists influence how people perceive themselves as well as how others see them. As special-effects makeup artist Jenn Blum says in a *Mental Floss* article, "Whether you want to look really scary or dead … or if you just want to be the best version of yourself, the fact that you can use makeup to do that is really exciting."

There are three phases of film production: preproduction, production, and postproduction. The preproduction phase covers everything that takes place before filming begins. Production, also called "principal filming," is the actual filming, and postproduction consists of the activities that take place after filming to complete the movie. Makeup artists and stylists work almost exclusively in the first two phases. The exception is digital makeup artists, who are called on to apply virtual makeup to actors in the postproduction phase.

Makeup and Styling in Preproduction

The key makeup artist (also called the makeup designer) and the hair designer are in charge of their departments. In preproduction, the makeup and hair designers must perform both creative and administrative tasks. Each makeup or hair job begins with the key makeup artist or stylist reading the script thoroughly, keeping in mind the director's concepts for the movie. They must also take into account the nature of the characters, including their personalities and relationships with each other. They meet with the director to discuss his or her requirements for the film or TV show. The key makeup artist and hair designer must work closely with each other and with the key costume designer, set designer, and lighting director over the course of filming to ensure that all the production elements come together to create the desired effect.

Once the key artists have a good feel for the production, they research elements of makeup and style for the location and time period, if necessary. They create a makeup and hair plot, which lists the makeup and hairstyles as they appear at the various points in the production. Next, they create sketches for the designs they propose to use throughout the production. Sketches might be created by hand or generated on a computer. Knowledge of makeup/ hairstyles in different cultures and historical periods is not the only requirement. The key artist also needs to understand how lighting can affect makeup in

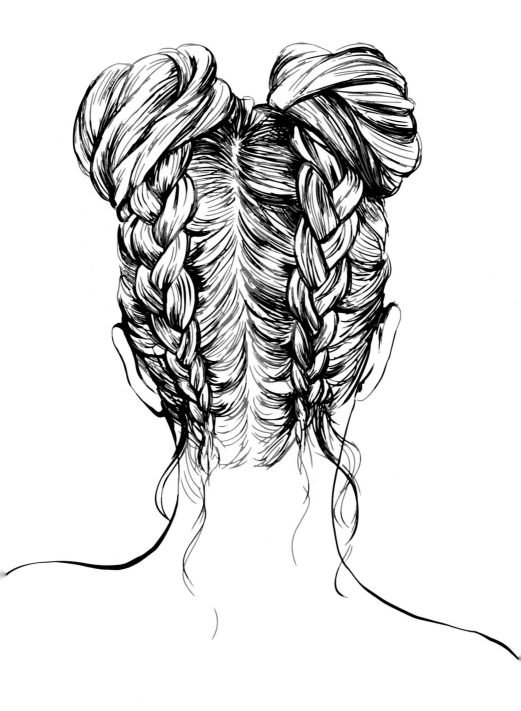

In the design phase, the key makeup artist sketches all the hairstyles to be created for each character.

order to choose particular colors and tones. During the design phase, he or she must consider the physical features of the actors and any problems that will have to be addressed—from allergies to flaws such as blemishes, scars, or tattoos. The degree of lighting must be considered, as well as the various types of lights used in film and video, which can change the colors of makeup and hair, making it paler, bluer, or redder, for example. The key designers present their sketches to the director for approval. Often changes are requested, so the designs are altered and again shown to the director.

Once the designs are approved by the director, the designers create an estimate of what it will cost to make up and style the cast of the film or show, for inclusion in the film or show's budget. The key makeup artist and hair designer must plan out what activities will be necessary and draw up a schedule for completing them. They must make sure that adequate tools and materials are on hand prior to the start of makeup and hair work. The key makeup artist also arranges appointments with optometrists and dentists for actors who require special contact lenses or dental prostheses. Once all prostheses, contact lenses, hairpieces, and the like are received, they are inventoried and stored until the department is ready to use them.

If special-effects makeup is required, it might be created in-house, or the key designer might hire a company that specializes in special-effects makeup, especially if practical special effects (components that work mechanically, such as eyes that rotate on stalks) are required. A studio might have a staff of makeup and hair artists and assistants, or it might hire freelancers for each project. Even if there is a permanent staff, additional artists might be required, especially on a large project with a lot of extras (also called background or atmosphere) who need to be made up.

If additional staff is needed, the key designers hire them. They also assign the work that each member of the staff will be responsible for. On a small film or show, the key artists might supervise the artists directly. On large projects, there will be a senior artist, whose job it is to oversee the artists doing the work, while the key artists concentrate on the administrative aspects of the project, such as tracking the budget and schedule and interfacing with the director and other department heads. If there is a senior artist, then the key artists must make sure that, prior to production, the senior artist fully understands the concepts for the makeup and any special issues that must be addressed. He or she is charged with making sure the makeup

A makeup artist places a bald cap over an actor's hair to provide a smooth surface on which to place special-effects makeup.

TOM SAVINI:
MASTER OF HORROR

Special-effects makeup artist Tom Savini attends the celebration of *The Walking Dead*'s one hundredth episode in 2017.

Tom Savini is best known for his horror special-effects makeup. Born in 1946 in Pittsburgh, Pennsylvania, he became fascinated with film makeup after viewing the 1957 movie *Man of a Thousand Faces*. From then on, he devoted himself to practicing monster makeup on himself and his friends. In his teens, he did makeup and monster design, on a volunteer basis, for *Chiller Theater* on a local Pittsburgh TV station.

His earliest professional work was in low-budget independent horror films. When Savini was a sophomore in high school, he met director George Romero when he came to Savini's school looking for actors for a film. Some years later, Savini applied to do the makeup on Romero's *Night of the Living Dead* and was hired, but he had to go to Vietnam instead. In a 2002 *Pittsburgh Post-Gazette* article, he says of his time in Vietnam, "I was a combat photographer. My job was to shoot images of damage to machines and to people. Through my lens, I saw some hideous [stuff]. To cope with it, I guess I tried to think of it as special effects."

A few years later, Romero invited Savini to do the makeup for the movie *Dawn of the Dead* by sending him a telegram that said simply, "Start thinking of ways to kill people." His work on the film gained him recognition in the industry.

Savini went on to do the special-effects makeup for *Friday the 13th* in 1980, one of the movies that popularized the "splatter film" genre (horror movies featuring lots of blood and gore). These films were just the start of a career that has lasted decades.

applied matches the agreed-upon style and design, and that continuity is maintained every day during shooting. Continuity means that every element remains the same from shot to shot.

Stylists don't just cut and style hair. At times they have to dye or bleach an actor's hair. In addition, wigs are often used in projects. The wigs are of very high quality so that they will look as natural as possible. They must be styled just like real hair.

Makeup and Styling During Production

When a production starts, the senior artists must make sure that anything needed by a certain time is ready and available, including special-effects makeup and wigs created in-house or purchased from outside sources.

When actors arrive at the studio, the first thing they do is visit the hair, makeup, and wardrobe departments. Makeup artists do the actual work of making actors' looks match the designs set for the movie, both applying and touching up the makeup. Assistant makeup artists perform lower-level tasks and help the makeup artists during makeup preparation and application.

Each day, makeup artists and stylists work from a schedule provided by the assistant director, which lists the scenes to be shot that day (often not in order of the script). The artists generally have their own kits containing the makeup they prefer to use. However, molding materials and larger tools such as airbrushing

A makeup artist and assistant paint a prosthesis, which has been molded and then applied to an actor's face.

equipment might be provided by the makeup and hair department. Makeup artists often make molds and use materials such as foam and latex to create particular prostheses required for the character.

The day begins earlier for makeup artists than for actors. The makeup and hair stylists must arrive on the set before dawn to prepare the supplies and equipment they require. They will rely on detailed notes, sketches, and photographs to create the desired makeup for the actors who have been assigned to them. Special-effects makeup—whether for aliens or burn

Here is an array of wigs for use in a film. Stylists must design, create, wash, and style wigs just like real hair.

victims—and age makeup can take hours to apply. It's usual for pre-filming makeup to begin in the wee hours of the morning so that actors can be ready to film when it is light.

In situations where heavy age makeup or special effects makeup is applied, filming often continues until late at night. Because of the time required to apply the makeup and the effect that wearing heavy makeup has on the actors' skin, it is desirable to get as much shooting as possible done at one time. Makeup and hair stylists must be on hand to do repairs and touch-ups as required.

When applying heavy makeup, adhesives, and rubber appliances, makeup artists have to be especially careful in cleaning and preparing actors' skin. Actors get to know particular makeup artists. If a star requests a particular artist to work on him or her, the chosen artist will be dedicated to that star, and other members of the team will work on the other actors.

As much as possible, directors try to arrange filming so that if a character's hair color has to change over the course of the film, all the scenes with one color are shot together. At times, however, this isn't possible, perhaps because of bad weather or the unavailability of another actor in the scene. In this case, the stylist may need to change the character's hair color back and forth.

During production the senior makeup artist and stylist make sure that the work produced by the makeup artists and stylists conforms to the requirements. They must ensure that continuity is maintained from day to day. Continuity means that if, for example, a character's hair is curled behind her

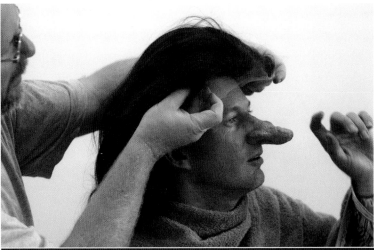

A stylist applies a wig. After it is in place, the hair must be arranged so that it looks natural on the character.

ear at the end of one scene, it is in the same position for the next scene, even if the scenes are shot out of order or on different days. Makeup and hair artists might snap photos of the actors after makeup/hair is completed so they can make sure it matches the next day. It is common for a makeup artist and stylist to be available on the set during shooting to fix makeup and hair, and change them as required from scene to scene.

Makeup artists and hair stylists have responsibilities after filming ends for the day. The makeup artist carefully removes the actors' makeup and returns prostheses to inventory. The stylist collects any wigs or hairpieces used by actors, washes them if necessary, and restyles them for the next day's shoot.

Makeup artists and stylists need to be sociable people as well as technicians and artists. They work intimately with actors for long periods when they apply makeup and style hair. It's natural for actors to talk with makeup artists and stylists during the process. It's particularly important to be sociable when applying makeup that is complex and possibly awkward to wear.

Postproduction: Digital Makeup

During postproduction, a film or TV show is edited. In this process, the film editor, working with the director, combines footage from the film, show, or shoot to create the final version. The only makeup artists involved during this phase are those who work digitally. Digital makeup artists use computer systems and software to alter the way actors look. Digital

A digital makeup artist electronically removes flaws from an actress's face frame by frame.

makeup artists might use technology to enhance the attractiveness of actors or to add additional features to special-effects makeup. There are two types of digital makeup: beauty work and special-effects makeup.

Making Beauty More Perfect

Beauty work takes place during the final phase of postproduction. Digital artists use special software to make actors look younger, thinner, and more muscular, "improving" their faces and bodies. The work is often performed by visual-effects studios that specialize in the process. One impetus for postproduction beauty work was the creation of high-definition (HD) film and television. Higher definition means that more detail is visible on the screen, with the result that audiences can see even tiny flaws and blemishes, especially in extreme close-ups. Digital makeup can remove tiny flaws that would otherwise show up in HD.

The technique is also useful in situations where an actor in her twenties is playing a teenager and needs to look especially youthful. One striking application of this technology was Lola Visual Effects' making Brad Pitt age backward—from old to young—in the 2008 film *The Curious Case of Benjamin Button.* At one point Pitt—in his forties—had to appear in a dance studio looking as if he were in his twenties, and digital makeup made this possible.

Actors have begun demanding that studios routinely use the technology to enhance their appearance in postproduction, and it has become a standard item in film budgets. The process is used to slim down actors, tighten loose skin around the neck and on the upper arms, and flatten bulging bellies—as well as make hair fuller and teeth unnaturally white. The software used by digital makeup artists allows them to move skin around and alter the shape of a face or body. The downside is that each frame of the film has to be retouched individually, so the process is time-consuming and expensive.

Aging an actor is just as painstaking a process as making someone look younger. Digital artists need to understand the changes that occur as a person ages. People don't just get wrinkles. The eyes spread farther apart, the hairline recedes, skin sags, and earlobes get longer. One caveat of the extensive use of beauty work is that normal people, especially young people, should

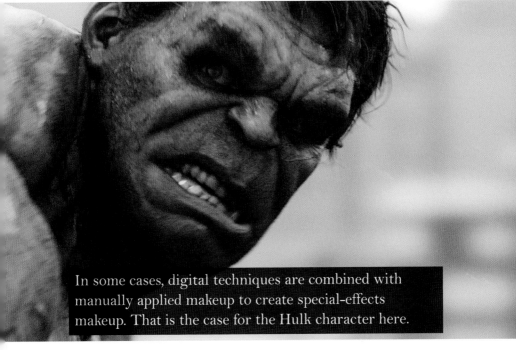

In some cases, digital techniques are combined with manually applied makeup to create special-effects makeup. That is the case for the Hulk character here.

be aware that the ideal of beauty they see on the big and small screen is not real. In real life, even famous actors have imperfect bodies and faces.

Enhancing Special-Effects Makeup

Special courses are available that teach the skills needed to digitally enhance physical special-effects makeup once a film or video is completed, as well as the skills for creating completely digital creatures and characters. Software programs that can be used for this purpose include ZBrush, Adobe Photoshop, and Creature Design as of 2018.

MastersFX is one special-effects studio that provides special-effects makeup enhancement services. They combine digital makeup with manually created

Students can practice makeup and styling by making their own videos or films. Here, a group of students in France makes their own film.

creature makeup in order to make more realistic and expressive creatures. In this approach, physical makeup in the form of prostheses or a mask is applied to an actor. After the scene is shot, computer technology is used to make the makeup appear more realistic. The goal is to enhance the performance of actors wearing prostheses rather than replace them with digital characters. The latter approach would require the other actors to react to a physical marker placed where the digital creature would later be inserted. This approach tends to elicit a less effective performance than having the actors interact with an actual person—or alien—because people have natural psychological responses to a living being that they don't demonstrate when facing inanimate objects. Thus, using a real actor results in more natural and expressive interactions.

The Canadian TV series *Falling Skies* is an example of a show that uses both physical makeup and digital visual effects. Combining physical and digital makeup effects requires the sculptor, lighting designer, cameraman, and actors to work together. The alien character Cochise in *Falling Skies* is filmed on the set with fully detailed practical prostheses. The actor's ability to move his face is limited by the makeup, but he can still interact with the other actors, sets, and props. Digital effects are added after live filming, during postproduction. They are used to make Cochise's eyes, eyebrows, facial muscles, and lips move as he peers around and speaks. Johnathan Banta, senior visual effects supervisor in the dMFX (digital makeup effects) division of MastersFX, says, "Our finished product looks real—because it is real. We enhance what is there."

Developing Makeup and Styling Skills

The best way to gain skill in makeup and styling is by practicing. Outlets such as YouTube have revolutionized the video industry by making it possible for anyone to create and upload his or her work. There are two sides to this coin. On the positive side, if your video catches on, or goes viral, and people are impressed with your work, you can gain a reputation that can help you move into a professional career. The downside is that if your work is not impressive, people will let you know.

In college, you will have the opportunity to work on student-made films as well as video. This type of experience will give you a sense, on a small scale, of what it is like to work on a film or television production. Both avenues allow you to practice your makeup and styling skills. Film and video are not the only ways you can hone your skills, however. Most high schools put on one or more plays during the year. Community theater groups also mount productions. Volunteering to do makeup for school and community theater productions gives you valuable practice, especially in the area of beauty and historical makeup

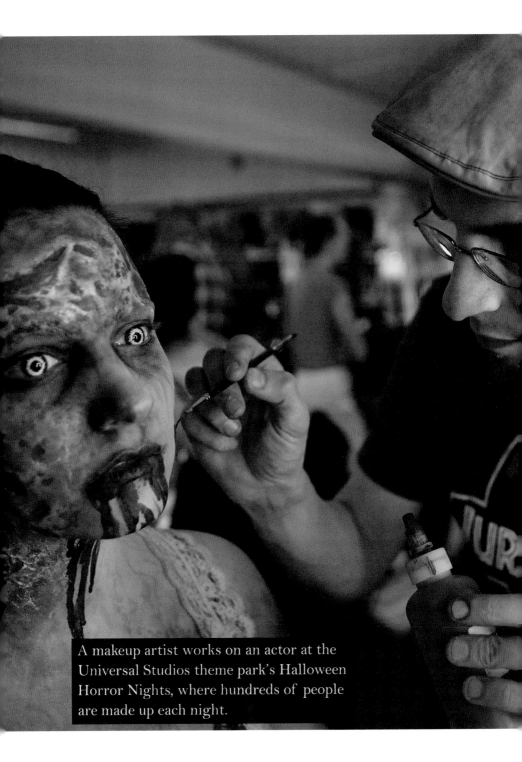

A makeup artist works on an actor at the Universal Studios theme park's Halloween Horror Nights, where hundreds of people are made up each night.

and hairstyling. Although many students become involved in makeup because they are interested in doing special effects work, that is not the only style of makeup used in films and TV shows. In order to obtain a professional job, it is beneficial to have the widest possible range of skills. In addition, if you want to work in a studio makeup department, you will need the range of skills that allow you to work on any type of film the studio may produce and assign you to.

Working on local theater and video projects allows you to gain experience in working with actors and directors as well. It will teach you how to interpret the director's descriptions of the requirements for the actors' makeup and hair, and how to produce renderings for approval. You will learn how to interact with actors when applying makeup, how to deal with problems during filming, and how to work to a schedule. You can volunteer to do makeup and styling for theatrical productions by contacting the person who directs plays at your school. You can locate community theaters in your area by checking "community theater" and your town's name on the internet. You can then contact the director of the group to volunteer.

If you are interested in doing special-effects makeup, experience is key to getting an entry-level position in this competitive field. You can easily start while in high school by working on student films and videos, but there are a number of other outlets that use special-effects makeup. One of the most common is seasonal venues such as haunted houses. Well before the holiday starts, check online for "haunted house" followed by your state's name, then contact the director of the project in your area to see if he or she can use a makeup artist. Don't restrict yourself to Halloween, however. Many towns and private organizations create special performances for other holidays such as Christmas and Easter.

You can also participate in makeup competitions. They are fun, allow you to see what other makeup artists are doing, and give you a chance to make contacts with professionals who judge the contest. You might also obtain projects to work on as a volunteer or trainee.

To find out about the tools of the trade and the latest techniques used in makeup, visit trade shows such as the International Makeup Artists Trade Show (IMATS), which holds shows at various cities in the United States and Canada as well as other international locations. The show is open to members of the public at least sixteen years old. You can also subscribe to trade magazines such as *Make-Up Artist Magazine* and *Modern Salon.*

Makeup and Styling Internships

The best way to develop both experience and contacts in the makeup and styling industries is through internships. Internships are unpaid positions that allow a student to learn on the job. You can start to apply for part-time or summer internships while in high school. Participating in part-time and summer internships is critical during college. Film and television are industries where entry-level jobs are often obtained as a result of personal contacts. So applying for as many internships as possible during your school years can make a significant difference when you apply for your first job.

Doing production of films and television shows is demanding. It is a field in which deadlines are often tight and hours are long. Taking on an internship gives you an opportunity to observe how professionals handle the job and can help you decide if the career is right for you. Interns perform very basic support tasks for the professionals on set. Despite the fact that you are not performing the creative tasks, an internship provides an excellent opportunity to learn the details of what makeup artists and stylists do in the real world. It teaches you not only how to apply your skills but also to recognize the areas where you lack expertise and need to learn more. As an intern, you can learn new skills as well as tricks of the trade. Interns have the opportunity to meet and impress industry professionals. It's important to get contact information from everyone you meet. Such contacts could be useful in the future when you look for a job or job reference.

Internships can be located by searching entertainment employment websites and makeup and beauty industry organizations' websites. Entertainment industry trade publications, such as *Variety*, provide information on new film and television projects on which production is going to start. One can contact the head of makeup or styling and ask if there is a position for an intern. When applying for an internship, you need to send a résumé and a cover letter explaining your interest in the makeup or styling industry and your willingness to learn more about the field. Your cover letter should emphasize the contribution you can make to the team.

The film and TV industries are small worlds. Being an intern is your chance to make a good impression on industry professionals. Therefore, how you conduct yourself on the job is important. Both when you are an intern and when you get your first job, the following characteristics will increase your chances of getting further work.

Be professional. Show up on time; be positive, helpful, and polite. Do not act arrogant or brag about people you know or have worked with.

Work hard. Don't wait to be assigned work. If you don't have work to do, ask what you can do to help. Learn as much as you can, and if you don't know how to do something, ask. Do your best work, and if you make a mistake, admit it and correct it, or ask for help in doing so. Even though you are not being paid, you are part of a team doing real work, and being a productive team member can lead to more work in the future.

Each makeup artist must have a kit that contains a variety of makeup, like eyeshadows and blushes, and tools, such as brushes.

CHAPTER FOUR

Challenges and Missteps

All types of problems can arise when preparing makeup during the production of a film or TV show. Some types of problems can be anticipated. Others are unpredictable. Each production will have its own unique issues. However, there are some typical challenges that arise in the course of working as a makeup artist or stylist. Some of these problems are technical, and others are professional.

Difficulties Getting Started

The first problem a new makeup artist or stylist faces is getting work. There is a great deal of competition for makeup and stylist jobs in film and television. As with many other creative fields, reaching the point where one has steady work or is hired in a permanent position requires a great deal of determination and persistence. Often young artists have to work another job on the side until they are able to find regular makeup work. A makeup artist or stylist who works on a freelance basis, even after he or she starts getting regular work, will have to continuously self-promote,

Working as a freelance or part-time hairdresser in a salon can allow one to take on movie or TV work when it is available.

endeavor to make industry contacts, and look for upcoming projects.

At first, a makeup artist does not start out creating the fabulous creatures displayed on films and TV shows. An aspiring makeup artist generally spends about two years working as a trainee or makeup assistant. It's important for people not to limit themselves early in their career. Many people want to become makeup artists because they want to do a particular type of makeup, most commonly special-effects makeup. However, the best way to both obtain work and succeed on the job is to learn to work with as many types of makeup as possible, and with as many types of media as you can.

Most makeup artists, even those with formal education, learn many of their skills on the job. Trying to learn different types of skills early in their career allows them to apply for a broad range of projects and positions. It also allows them to make a greater number of contacts in film and television.

Makeup and hair trainees must be aware of their responsibilities. Makeup trainees must have a basic makeup kit, and entry-level stylists are expected to have appropriate styling tools. Entry-level artists don't start their careers working with stars. They do mostly support work. When they do makeup/styling, it is most likely to be working on extras, especially when there are a lot of background actors needed.

Activities performed by entry-level staff include:

- Supplying the department workstations with necessary materials, tools, and equipment prior to the start of work.

- Making notes about the details of makeup and hair to ensure continuity from shot to shot.

- Restocking supplies.

- Cleaning.

- Assisting the artists as necessary with everything from fetching supplies to helping finish a paint job on schedule.

- Applying makeup/styling actors, especially extras.

One important activity that entry-level artists and stylists do is create a portfolio of their work so they can demonstrate their capabilities. They document their work by keeping a log of the projects they've worked on and with whom. They take photos for their portfolio, if that is allowed.

As makeup artists and hair stylists progress in their profession, they become responsible for working on bigger stars. There can be an advantage to working with young actors starting out, however. Just as makeup artists and stylists move up the ladder, so do actors. It's not unusual for a makeup artist or hair stylist to start out working with unknown actors whose careers later take off. When that happens, not only will having done their makeup enhance the artist's career prospects, but if the actor likes and respects the work the makeup artist or stylist has done for them in the past, they might request that person on future projects. Since makeup and hair play such a large role in an actor's career, contributing to an actor's success can be a great source of satisfaction and recognition.

Getting an Education

One mistake that many aspiring makeup artists and stylists make is assuming that being creative is enough to make one successful. In fact, it is necessary to learn technical skills. Hair stylists are required in most states to attend a cosmetology school and be certified and licensed. The educational path for makeup artists isn't as set. Many makeup artists started by creating makeup and masks while they were in high school. There is no doubt a huge creative aspect to the makeup, but doing makeup on a professional level is as much science as art. Makeup artists need a broad range of skills. They need knowledge of anatomy, color theory, chemistry (to understand how materials work together—and don't), electronics if they are interested in special-effects makeup, the different types of equipment used in professional makeup, and in some cases digital visual effects techniques. They need to learn how to use different types of professional sculpting, painting, and molding techniques. They must understand how to keep makeup tools and brushes hygienic for the safety of the actors they work on. Skills can be learned on the job, but that takes much longer and means making more mistakes than getting a good foundation by attending a makeup school.

Most makeup artists and stylists find the first four to five years of their career difficult. This is a period that new artists spend learning. Getting a proper foundation can help young artists cut down on the time it takes to become proficient. Taking specialty programs or courses while working at an entry-level job can also enhance a candidate's job prospects. Programs that last from weeks to months, in areas such as wig-making, special effects, and digital visual effects, can make you a more desirable job candidate.

Working with Celebrities

One of the draws of being employed in the film and television industry is the chance to work with celebrities. While one does work with stars, the job isn't all glamour. It involves working with messy products for long hours applying makeup and styling hair, and then spending hours on set or on location— often outdoors—continuously fixing actors' makeup

Teachers in a special-effects workshop show students how to apply makeup to make a person look like a zombie.

and hair. The hard work is worth it to achieve a look that is striking onscreen as the result of their efforts.

When a makeup artist or stylist reaches the point of working with well-known actors, they are faced with a new set of challenges. They work intimately with actors for long periods. Being sociable makes the work more pleasant for both the artist and actor. However, they have to be wary of being too familiar—asking questions that are too personal. Sometimes, celebrities have preferences for certain products. Makeup artists and hair stylists try to accommodate actors' preferences as much as possible. However, they have to be tactfully insistent about using the proper products necessary to attain the look the director desires.

Early in their career, makeup artists and stylists will have to figure out the right balance between being accommodating and saying that something isn't a good approach—and how to do so tactfully. Often celebrities have a particular "look." When doing beauty makeup on such actors, makeup artists and stylists often look up recent photos and get a sense of what the actor likes. Most actors are professionals and respect other professionals. If a celebrity is extremely difficult to deal with, the artist or stylist might have to consult the senior makeup artist, makeup designer, or director.

Some makeup artists have reported experiencing sexual harassment or inappropriate sexual behavior from male actors. This activity is mostly directed toward women, but there have been incidents that also involved young men. Hollywood studios and professional television studios, as well as most subcontracted companies, have policies and procedures for dealing with sexual harassment. It is important for those in the profession to know what to do if they encounter a problem. Time's Up is an organization that fights both sexual harassment and the inequality of women in the entertainment industry. Their website contains detailed information on what a person can do after experiencing sexual harassment. The organization has established the Time's Up Legal Defense Fund to help women with legal cases stemming from sexual harassment. It is specifically designed for women in entertainment-industry positions who are not stars, as well as for women in other industries.

People of Color

As with other positions in the entertainment industry, people of color are underrepresented in both acting and production positions. It is important for makeup artists to be able to create perfect natural-looking makeup on African Americans and other people of color, not just white actors. However, white makeup artists have generally had less training and practice working on people of color. Therefore, they do not have exposure to the particular issues involved in making up people with other types of skin tones. In his article "5 Challenges Black and POC Makeup Artists Have to Deal With," makeup artist Victor Amos points out why some white makeup artists have difficulty mastering the full range of human complexions. He acknowledges that many white makeup artists can service people of any complexion, but explains that others cannot. Amos says:

This problem does not exist in a vacuum, however. There is a reason for the prevalence of white makeup artists who cannot service dark skin ... When you look at the racial demographics of American neighborhoods ... white people live near other white people, and black people live near other black people ... How does this manifest into disparities in makeup application ability? Easy. Think about how most of us learn our craft. The majority of us developed our talents by practicing on family and friends. White people will practice on other white people, and black people will practice on other black people.

Makeup artists need to be able to handle a broad range of complexions in order to apply appropriate makeup of the correct tone and color. Young makeup artists need to practice the skills of applying makeup to people of all ethnicities. For instance, when making student films or videos, they should try to incorporate a diverse cast to gain experience working on people with a variety of skin tones.

The movie and television industries have implemented initiatives to create more diversity in both cast and crew on productions. In 2016, the Academy of Motion Picture Arts and Sciences instituted new rules to encourage hiring more diverse casts, and actress and 2018 Academy Award winner Frances McDormand encouraged stars to include a document called the "inclusion rider" in their union contracts.

This document requires a film to hire both actors and production crew members who reflect the diversity of the population. An increased number of production positions might provide more opportunity for nonwhite makeup artists. An increasingly diverse population of actors means that makeup artists must become adept at providing makeup that enhances the look of actors of all backgrounds.

Taking Criticism

A major characteristic of successful makeup artists/ stylists is a thick skin. A makeup artist and hair stylist's work is seen by everyone—the other department members, the director, the actors, other crew members, the audience, reviewers, and so on. And every single person who sees it is going to have an opinion. Some will be positive. Some will be negative. No creative work is ever loved by everyone. So if you pursue a career in makeup and styling, you need to learn to take both positive and negative criticism in stride and differentiate between constructive and unconstructive comments. This is just as true of positive criticism as negative. If someone "just loves" your makeup but can't give any particular reason, that is not valuable feedback. A person who loves the way your edges are finished so that your prostheses look natural is giving you information on what works, and you should note that for the future. The reverse is also true. If someone "just hates" the look, that's pretty much meaningless unless he or she can point to specific elements that don't work. That person might hate that style of makeup, dislike the actor wearing the makeup, or need to write a snarky review because that's what the readers respond to. If someone says that some part of the makeup overpowers the actor's face and draws attention to itself in a way that distracts from the illusion, that's a point you should consider in the future. Either way, you need to realize that negative criticism is part of the job and not obsess over it.

Makeup Failure

Not all makeup is successful. Good makeup must be believable—even when it's created for a fantasy character. Sometimes makeup is so whimsical, exaggerated, or just plain inappropriate that it is unbelievable.

The makeup in some movies is deliberately outlandish. For instance, the characters who inhabit Wonderland in the 2010 version of *Alice in Wonderland*, Captain Jack Sparrow in the *Pirates of the Caribbean* movies, and the characters in the fantasy portion of the TV show *Once Upon a Time* wear distinct, over-the-top makeup, but it works because it looks believable on the actors and suits the tone of the film or TV show. But exaggerated makeup isn't always successful; sometimes, it is merely distracting. For example, the choice to use a large prosthetic nose on Nicole Kidman when she played the Virginia Woolf character in *The Hours* led some audiences to focus on it to the point of being distracted.

Above all, don't create racial stereotypes. Creating villainous or comic characters represents a particular challenge because it usually involves altering the actors' features. In the past, this often involved exaggerating racial features, such as slanted eyes. This is inappropriate and offensive. Makeup artists and stylists must be able to create a sense of villainy in characters without recourse to stereotyping. Rumpelstiltskin, one of the main villains in *Once Upon a Time*, and Lord Voldemort in *Harry Potter and the Deathly Hallows* are examples of villains that are scary but not stereotypical.

The Challenge of HD, IMAX, and 3D

Cinematic technologies such as HD, 3D movies, and IMAX have created challenges for makeup artists and stylists. HD technology has given film and TV higher resolution. This means that they show finer details. IMAX shows images in much larger scale than conventional movie screens, which again means that the audience can see more detail. 3D technology shows more of the actor. For instance, when looking at the side of an actor's head in 3D, it is possible to see part of the back of the head as well. Therefore, the makeup must be perfect the whole way around. Any seams, bumps, or imperfections will show.

When low resolution was the norm, actors' blemishes could be hidden by thick makeup and clever lighting. Now, not only is every wrinkle visible, but heavy makeup itself can be seen. For this reason, airbrushing has come to be used extensively to smooth out imperfections in both beauty and special effects

A makeup artist uses an airbrush to spray a fine layer of paint onto a prosthesis.

makeup. Airbrushing is a technique in which a thin spray is used to apply paint or makeup to the actor's skin, instead of a brush.

Another problem created by HD is that even products that aren't visible to the naked eye when applied, such as a setting powder used on top of makeup, can make skin appear dull and unrealistic in HD. Special powders designed for HD must be used to avoid such problems. In the past, television makeup artists could just check their work by viewing it in a mirror. The reflected image was a good approximation of how the actor would appear on the television screen. However, modern large-screen TVs present much the same problem as large movie screens. Every detail is visible, so the makeup requires a much closer examination.

BEWARE OF TOXIC MATERIALS

Stylists use chemicals to alter and set hair and attach hairpieces. Makeup artists use an even larger amount of chemicals—not only makeup but solvents, adhesives, paints, plastics, and other materials. The fumes from some of these chemicals can be unhealthy, the materials can harm skin and hair, and in some cases they can be flammable when combined. There have been numerous examples of actors suffering bad reactions to chemicals used in makeup.

Makeup artists and stylists need to find out if actors have any known allergies to ingredients, and if possible, use alternatives. They should also be thoroughly knowledgeable about the ingredients in the materials they use, and understand the effects of combining the chemicals they mix.

When Jennifer Lawrence undertook the role of Mystique in her first X-Men movie in 2011, the blue makeup gave her boils and blisters. She also worried that breathing the toxic fumes during the hours of painting required could cause permanent physical harm. In one article, Lawrence was quoted as saying, "I love these movies … It's just the paint … fumes and toxins … I can't even pronounce this and that's going in my nose? I'm breathing that?" (By the third movie, her character was hardly ever blue, because by then, she had the clout to refuse to submit to the process.)

In another example of a makeup problem, a makeup crew failed to adequately consider what would happen when the makeup they were using on the face of actor Kuno Becker was combined with water. In one scene, water was thrown on him, which caused his makeup to run into his eyes—and the chemicals in it nearly blinded him. Becker publicly accused the makeup department of not taking the trouble to learn what chemicals were in the makeup they used.

Hair treatments can involve dangerous chemicals too. In 2013, actress Jennifer Aniston was forced to cut her hair short after it was damaged by a hair-straightening treatment that used the chemical formaldehyde (used to preserve dead bodies).

In addition to being knowledgeable about the materials they work with, makeup artists and stylists need to learn to recognize the signs of a serious problem, such as an allergic reaction or difficulty breathing. Also, they need to protect themselves adequately when dealing with chemicals to avoid injuring themselves.

Working with Negative Space

Makeup is applied on top of an actor's face. A special issue presents itself when a disfigured character is missing flesh from his or her face. Before HD, IMAX, and 3D, makeup artists could create a realistic effect of missing flesh by putting prostheses and makeup on top of the actor's skin. The problem now is how to create the illusion of negative space (a hole from which material has been removed). In his third film, *The Box*, director Richard Kelly was faced with this problem.

A central character in the film is a mysterious visitor, Arlington Steward, played by Frank Langella. He is a burn victim and is missing a large portion of flesh on the left side of his head. Because he was portraying a central character, Langella needed to be physically present for his scenes. His character could not just be inserted into the film digitally, as is sometimes done with minor characters, such as Grand Moff Tarkin in *Star Wars: Rogue One*, who was previously played by actor Peter Cushing. (By the time *Rogue One* was filmed, Cushing was deceased.)

To make matters worse, many of Langella's scenes went on for an extended period, allowing plenty of time for the audience to observe his face. Kelly didn't have the $100 million budget that would have allowed him to do a postproduction frame-by-frame alteration of the character's face. Langella was in 144 shots, so the issue was how to perform the digital portion of his alteration cost-effectively. The solution was to use a combination of digital and physical makeup, provided by the visual-effects firm Gradient Effects. Some makeup and prostheses were applied directly to

Langella's face, and then the look was enhanced using computer graphics technology.

The digital effects makeup team's clever solution used optical motion-capture on set to add the computer-generated portion to the film. Optical motion capture is most familiar as the technology used to create characters in video games. A video camera is used to record an actor as he or she performs the actions of the fictional character. The image is sent to a computer, where the details of the actor's face, body, and clothing are altered to those of the character. In Langella's case, Gradient Effects used four cameras in addition to the ones used for regular filming. These cameras were focused on Langella, tracking the position of his face. They were connected to a computerized system that allowed animation to be created while filming was taking place. The result was film that included a digital version of Langella's face with the flesh missing. Thus, he could physically act on the set with the other characters during filming, and the finished film didn't need expensive frame-by-frame alteration in postproduction.

When Things Go Wrong

One of the problems faced by film and television makeup artists and stylists is the stress of working under pressure. This is especially true in the special-effects makeup area. The work hours can be long—sometimes fourteen to sixteen hours a day. It is inevitable that no matter how perfectly a team plans or schedules, there will be problems. Prostheses won't always be perfect when removed from molds, paint won't look right, chemicals mixed together won't work as expected, pieces won't fit, special effects components that worked fine in the workshop will fail to function on set—the list goes on. Each problem puts the team farther behind.

When things go wrong, a team's members are prone to get upset and frustrated and snap at anyone around, including the makeup artists and stylists. And they are not just working with members of the makeup and styling teams, or even just the makeup and hair designer. Other people, such as the production supervisor and director, could become concerned—and these people can affect the artists' present and future employment. Early in a makeup artist's or stylist's career, when working on a professional film or TV project, they won't be the person in charge of the department, so they shouldn't have to deal with the production supervisor or director directly. However, if the makeup/hair designer gets called on the carpet because of a problem, he or she will feel pressured and might put more pressure on the artists as a result.

The same issues apply when you are working on YouTube or student film projects. If you are working on a small-scale project, such as these, you might well be the go-to person responsible for makeup/hair. Therefore, you need to know how to handle people when problems arise.

To make matters worse, the people on the production crew are not the only people working long hours. Actors also have to prepare in the early hours of the morning and work all day and often into the evening. They too become tired and testy. The first thing makeup artists and stylists need to learn is to remain calm when things go wrong, so they can focus on fixing the problem. They also have to be able to step back and not take things personally. This is not always easy when an annoyed supervisor, director, or actor shouts or snaps at them. Whatever happens, they must be careful not to shout or snap back, but realize that the person is upset, worried, and possibly tired as well. Often the best approach is simply to let the person finish speaking, then calmly explain that they understand the issue and that the problem will be addressed. Often when dealing with people who are irritable, just letting them vent alleviates much of the tension from the situation. Maintaining a controlled demeanor when things go wrong serves several purposes: it makes a professional appear reliable, someone who remains steady in the face of problems; it defuses an emotionally overwrought situation rather than escalating it, which allows everyone to work together to solve problems; and it gains an artist or stylist respect.

It's important to maintain a sense of perspective. Yes, the project might take longer than expected and additional costs might be incurred, but these things happen in every production, and directors and producers—no matter how they respond—are used to dealing with them. Having to cope with problems is never fun. However, solving problems—or even seeing how they are solved—is an important skill. Next time, they'll know how to handle that problem. More importantly, they gain experience in handling people when a problem occurs.

Makeup/styling skills used in film or TV
can apply to fields like fashion modeling.

CHAPTER FIVE

Applying Skills to Other Jobs

Some film and television makeup artists and stylists will remain in that profession for their entire career. They may move up in the makeup department hierarchy or become freelance designers. Most experienced makeup artists and stylists who leave the entertainment industry remain in the makeup/ styling field. Some will become freelance makeup artists specializing in providing beauty makeup to celebrities. Others will leave film or television work to start their own makeup- or hair-related businesses. Digital graphic artists working as digital makeup artists can often find work in related industries such as the video game or animation fields. Those most likely to change from makeup/styling to other fields are young artists who decide the field is not for them.

The reverse is also true. Many makeup artists and stylists started their careers by working in salons or selling cosmetics to the public. They then used their knowledge of products and techniques to move to makeup/stylist positions in the entertainment industry. So, for those who are not able to find an entertainment industry job directly out of school, this is one route to consider.

Alternate Careers

The following are some fields that film and television makeup artists and stylists switch to.

Fashion, Advertising, and Public Relations

Fashion designers rely on makeup artists and hair stylists to create the look of the models in their fashion shows. Advertising and public relations agencies, as well as fashion magazines, hire professional photographers to take photographs of models. The photographers need professional makeup artists and stylists to prepare models. As in film and TV work, the process starts with meeting the designer or photographer and understanding his or her vision. Fashion shows can involve many models who must be prepared in a short amount of time. Photo shoots usually involve only one or a few models. Most of the makeup artists and stylists who work on these types of projects do so on a freelance basis, being called in by clients when they have a project. The advantage of freelance work, especially for an established makeup artist, is the ability to set one's own schedule. The disadvantages are that the individual has to continually find new projects, and they are responsible for keeping track of business expenses and providing their own "benefits," such as health and disability insurance.

Celebrity Makeup/Hairstyling

Celebrity makeup artists and hair stylists work exclusively for one or more celebrity clients. They do

Beauty makeup/styling is used to make a model look striking for a photo shoot.

their makeup for public appearances, photo shoots, and any presence on television talk and interview shows. However, they don't just work on film and TV stars. They apply their skills to recording artists, top models, and politicians as well.

Cosmetics

Unless they have been running their own company or worked in the cosmetics industry prior to switching to the entertainment industry, makeup artists and stylists won't have business experience. Therefore, when they look for a business job, they often choose to apply for work at businesses closely related to makeup or styling, such as cosmetics or hair products companies, where their makeup/styling experience gives them an edge. They might choose to work for a cosmetics company whose products are sold to consumers, salons and spas, or professional makeup artists/stylists. Another option is to work on a personal care product line in a large consumer products company with multiple lines of business.

How much experience a person has in the makeup/styling field has an effect on what type of job he or she can obtain. Positions in these companies range from sales and marketing to brand or project management. A brand manager is responsible for the packaging design, marketing, advertising, and distribution of a particular brand. He or she works with personnel in a variety of departments, including development, production, sales and marketing, and finance. Professionals in makeup and hairstyling have an understanding of what aspects of a product appeal to clients and how to communicate with them, which are advantages when looking for a job in this area.

Other Businesses

Makeup artists and hair stylists sometimes choose to open their own businesses. Hair stylists might open a salon. Makeup artists might open their own special effects or visual special effects (vFX) companies. Some of these companies provide services to the film and television industries as subcontractors. Others go beyond film and television to provide services to other organizations, such as those in the video game industry, theme parks, or attractions like haunted houses. Some successful makeup artists/stylists have become entrepreneurs, creating their own lines of products. One example is Eugenia Weston, who did makeup for celebrities such as Bette Midler and Michelle Pfeiffer before she started Senna Cosmetics.

Starting a company requires more than talent. To be successful, the individual needs to understand finance, marketing, human resources, and other business disciplines. Therefore, before embarking on this path, it's a good idea to take some courses in these areas. Even if the entrepreneur hires professionals to handle the administrative activities of the operation, such knowledge is beneficial because it allows him or her to understand and respond to business issues.

Preparing for Real-World Careers

When starting out in a makeup or styling career in the entertainment industry, many people work on a freelance or part-time basis while working at a regular day job. It can be advantageous to try to find a job in a related field. Salons and spas hire hair stylists with flexible hours. Another option is to provide services on a freelance basis doing stylist/beauty makeup work for brides, photographers, or fashion showrooms, which not only provides more income but also gives the person valuable material for his or her résumé and portfolio. A career in other areas of the entertainment industry or in a field outside of the entertainment industry is also a possibility. The following are skills that makeup artists and stylists develop that can help them in any career they choose to pursue.

Teamwork

As makeup artists and stylists in film or TV, a person learns to work as part of a team. They understand how to present ideas to others and how to compromise to arrive at a vision that the team can move forward with. They know how to work collaboratively when problems occur, focusing on solutions. They have learned how to show that they respect and value the contributions of other team members, which, in turn, gains them respect and support. These same aspects of teamwork on projects apply to work outside the entertainment industry.

Project Skills

Businesses today are focused on running activities as "projects." These efforts incorporate a range of team members, often from different departments, and have an end goal and short-term goals that must be accomplished along the way. Whether people work at a makeup or styling job outside the entertainment industry or in another field altogether, they will find themselves calling on the project management skills they have developed. They will meet with a client or senior manager to learn what is required. They will then have to analyze the assignment to identify the tools, materials, people, and other resources needed. They might need to work with other people to complete the project. They will have to accomplish tasks according to a schedule, tracking their progress and sharing information with other members of the team to ensure that the project is accomplished on time.

Requirements may change over the course of the project. These changes mean it will be necessary to make adjustments to the schedule, and team members will have to accommodate the changes to their work. As with a film or TV production, they will have a budget with which they need to comply, meeting expectations for the finished result within that constraint. This will mean finding ways to meet the technical requirements without exceeding the budget.

These skills are not just the province of professional makeup artists and stylists. Working on your own videos or those of other students and participating in independent film work are excellent ways to hone your resourcefulness and learn how to use workarounds (a means of solving a problem with whatever materials are available) when you don't have extensive resources, since these projects often operate on shoestring budgets.

Interpersonal Skills

Makeup artists and stylists often encounter people who have strong personalities—and a stronger desire for recognition. Some of them will be extremely fussy, some will be hard to please, some will be demanding— and it's not just actors that fall into this category. It includes directors, designers, and producers as well. Outside of the entertainment industry, it's just as necessary to cope with difficult people, including superiors and customers or clients. People who choose to pursue this as a career will probably have developed the skills to calm down a person who is upset and refocus the conversation on how to solve the problem.

Stressful situations arise in businesses when problems occur and deadlines are tight. Makeup artists, especially those who have worked in special effects, have a great deal of experience in coping with this type of situation. The makeup and styling fields, especially in the entertainment industry, develop people-handling skills. Professionals must be able to control their emotions, reassure people that they are taking others' points of view into account, present their viewpoint tactfully, and gain others' trust and respect.

Makeup artists and stylists are likely to work with individuals with a wide range of backgrounds and ethnicities. Developing sensitivity to and the ability to work with different types of people is necessary to be successful in any field. In businesses outside the entertainment industry, professionals have to deal with people in many types of jobs and from various educational, ethnic, racial, and socioeconomic backgrounds. A makeup artist or stylist has to maintain a sense of empathy with those he or she works on and with. The people skills gained from being a makeup artist or stylist can give any professional a better understanding of clients/customers. This ability to identify what clients want or need will be valuable in any field where it is necessary to make sales or establish long-term relationships with clients.

One of the key elements of success in business is the ability to communicate clearly and effectively. This is especially true when dealing with managers outside one's own department, who will have their own concerns and agendas. Makeup artists and stylists are used to working with other experts such as those in costuming,

Teambuilding skills learned by makeup artists/stylists help when working on business projects.

lighting, and set design. They are experienced in working toward a consensus so that the project as a whole hangs together.

Creativity

Creativity, the ability to think of new and unique products and approaches, can be a key component of success. Creativity is certainly a benefit when a person has to create a presentation, produce a special event, solve a problem, or come up with a business strategy to achieve a goal. Businesses, regardless of industry, need to stay current with the trends in their field and develop new ideas to stay ahead of their competitors. A 2014 study by the business research consulting company Forrester Consulting showed that 82 percent of companies that fostered creativity had higher revenues and greater market share than their competitors. The report deemed creativity to be "essential to building brands, attracting buyers, and forging unique bonds with customers," as well as driving innovation.

Makeup artists and stylists know how to think creatively. Those who are willing to take risks and not just follow the same path as everyone else are more likely to come up with ideas that move a project or company forward. Creative people think outside the box and come up with new solutions to problems.

Interviewees in the Forrester report said that encouraging creativity allowed them to "get products to market faster, enjoy a price premium from buyers, have more people who speak on their behalf, and disrupt their traditional markets with new ideas and approaches."

Creative individuals are able to get to know their audience, understand their needs, and address their concerns. They leverage this understanding to develop engaging products and experiences that influence both present and potential customers by making them see things from a different perspective. This role corresponds to what makeup artists and stylists do on films and in television.

Hard Work and Persistence

Those employed in makeup and styling in the entertainment industry are used to working hard, often for long hours and under strict deadlines. Engaging in this type of performance helps them become successful at other jobs, when it is necessary to meet schedules or work outside of regular business hours. Since the hours are not likely to be as long per day as those in film and television work, they will present no difficulty for those coming from the entertainment industry.

Although makeup artists and stylists work as part of a team, each is responsible for his or her individual contribution to a project. They are experienced at working independently and having their part of the work done when it is needed. They also develop a habit of persistence. Obtaining work in the field and continuing to be hired for projects requires them to continuously seek out and pursue opportunities until they succeed. This attitude goes a long way in any job. It is particularly useful in sales jobs.

The techniques makeup artists and stylists develop to cope with the stress of long hours and upcoming deadlines apply equally well in other types of work. Those in the entertainment industry are used to the unexpected problems that frequently arise and are prepared to deal with them. Handling pressure well helps a person maintain good relationships with other team members and impresses clients and superiors— qualities that are valuable in any enterprise.

Time Management Skills

Time management skills are the key to completing all the tasks required to achieve a desired end result by a deadline. In the entertainment industry, makeup artists and stylists constantly work under time pressure. Shooting will take place at a set time, and everything must be completed by that point. Problems must be resolved so that everything is ready, and personnel must be able to quickly fix problems that arise during shooting. There are likely many actors whom makeup

GUESS WHO WORKED IN MAKEUP/STYLING

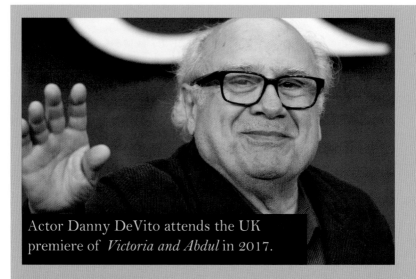

Actor Danny DeVito attends the UK premiere of *Victoria and Abdul* in 2017.

Some surprising people have worked in the makeup and styling industry before going on to become celebrities in their own right. Among them is actor Danny DeVito. Born in Asbury Park, New Jersey, DeVito never planned to become an actor. When he graduated from high school in 1962, at the age of nineteen, he didn't know what he wanted to do, so he took up his sister's offer to become a hairdresser in the salon she owned. He enjoyed working as a hairdresser. After a year, he decided he wanted to study professional makeup. He enrolled at the American Academy of Dramatic Arts in Manhattan, New York, to study makeup artistry. While at the academy, he became fascinated with acting and started taking acting classes. Once he started getting laughs for his comic acting, he was hooked and switched from makeup to acting.

Another actor who worked in makeup before becoming a success was Whoopi Goldberg. When she was a young single mother, Goldberg went to cosmetology school, and she is a licensed beautician. After having had several unrelated jobs, she answered an ad in the newspaper for a makeup artist—in a mortuary. She got the position and did makeup and hair on the corpses. In an interview on *Oprah's Master Class*, she says of working in a funeral home, "It's a rough gig … You have to be a certain kind of person. And you have to love people in order to make them worthy of a great send-off."

Whoopi Goldberg attends a screening of *Black Panther* in 2018.

artists/stylists need to prepare for a shoot, and professionals must constantly multitask.

These factors mean that stylists and makeup artists develop time management techniques. They learn to break projects down into tasks and assign them priorities. They know how to delegate tasks to assistants. This allows them to concentrate on the most important task or person. They have experience keeping track of the progress of projects and supervising those who work under them. In business, many managers don't give employees the freedom to work on their own, instead trying to manage all phases of work. However, employees are likely to work with more commitment and be more content and loyal when a manager empowers them by showing that he or she trusts them by delegating.

Makeup artists work in an environment that is often busy and sometimes chaotic. They can work well in situations where they are faced with interruptions, distractions, and requests for help from others. Having worked in a high-pressure business, makeup artists and stylists know the importance of scheduling time for themselves and providing themselves with recovery time, even when they are busy. It's easy for employees to let a job become their whole life, whether they are in the entertainment industry or in some other line of work. Balancing the demands of work with those of family, school, or other activities, while also caring for oneself will stand a person in good stead in any profession.

Representing the Company

Makeup artists and stylists have to deal extensively with people. They must be able to communicate with all the actors in a production, from extras to celebrities. This experience can be valuable when they have to put on business or sales presentations for customers, clients, or senior management. They know how to put people at ease and how to deal with people with sensitive egos. They have also learned how to overcome people's concerns about particular products. They are well suited to represent a company at large corporate events, such as a trade show exhibit or special event.

Being a makeup artist or stylist can be demanding, but it is a creative and fulfilling job. In this type of work the makeup artist or stylist has the opportunity to transform people and contribute to a production that will affect audiences. This can provide a great deal of satisfaction, despite the hard work required. It also provides a way to learn a variety of skills that can be used to enhance a person's chances of success in another type of business or profession.

GLOSSARY

adhesive Another name for glue.

airbrush A tool that sprays a fine mist of paint or makeup.

anatomy The physical structure of the body.

appliance A device or prosthesis applied to an actor's face.

aspire To want to achieve.

backlot The area behind a studio that contains buildings and outdoor areas in which films and TV shows are shot.

blemish A flaw.

caveat A warning or caution.

close-up A shot of an actor's face.

continuity Ensuring that details are identical from scene to scene in a film or video.

cosmetology The study of makeup and how to apply it.

entrepreneur A person who starts his or her own business.

expressive Showing emotion.

high definition (HD) A technology that shows a high degree of detail in an image or on a screen.

impetus Motivation.

kit The collection of tools and materials used by a makeup artist.

persistence Making a continuous effort.

portfolio A collection of photographs showing the work a person has done.

practical special effect A component of special-effects makeup that operates mechanically.

proficient Skilled.

property An original script, series concept, or a novel or work from another media.

prosthesis A shaped piece of plastic, latex, foam rubber, or other material glued to an actor's skin to change the look of his or her face.

sociable Friendly.

solvent A chemical that dissolves other materials.

subcontract To hire a company to perform work on a project.

visual special effects (vFX) Special effects created digitally.

FOR MORE INFORMATION

Books

Davis, Gretchen. *The Hair Stylist Handbook: Techniques for Film and Television.* New York: Focal Press, 2016.

Davis, Gretchen, and Mindy Hall. *The Makeup Artist Handbook: Techniques for Film, Television, Photography, and Theatre.* New York: Routledge, 2017.

Debreceni, Todd. *Special Makeup Effects for Stage and Screen: Making and Applying Prosthetics.* Burlington, MA: Focal Press, 2013.

McLean, Adrienne L., ed. *Behind the Silver Screen: Costume, Makeup, and Hair.* New Brunswick, NJ: Rutgers University Press, 2016.

Terry, Patricia L., and Gary Christensen. *Leading Ladies of Makeup Effects: Showcasing the Award-Winning Women of Makeup Effects for Film and Television.* Laguna Beach, CA: One Off Publishing, 2017.

Websites

CyberCollege: "Makeup for Film and Television"
http://cybercollege.com/makeup.htm
The CyberCollege website provides detailed information on working as a makeup artist in film and television.

***Makeup Artist* Magazine**
https://makeupmag.com
Makeup Artist magazine provides a wide range of online articles.

Make-Up Artists and Hair Stylists Guild
http://www.local706.org
The website of the official makeup artists and hair stylists' union for those working in films provides articles of subjects of interest as well as information on joining the guild.

Videos

"Anatomy of a TV Hit: CSI: Makeup and Special Effects Makeup"
https://www.youtube.com/watch?v=U5KhBltNFlw
Makeup Department Head Melanie Levitt for the TV series *CSI* provides an in-depth look at how her crew and Academy-Awarding-winning special-effects makeup artist Matthew Mungle create the makeup for the show.

"Special Effects Makeup: How Movie Monsters Are Made"
https://www.youtube.com/watch?v=Bax9LAXej4A
Special effects makeup artist Howard Berger, who did the makeup for *The Chronicles of Narnia*, shows how he creates movie monsters.

Online Articles

Brewer, Kirstie. "Making Up *The Walking Dead*: 'Growing Up I Wanted to Make Monsters.'" *Guardian*. March 22, 2016. https://www. theguardian.com/careers/2016/mar/22/monsters-horror-makeup-artist-walking-dead-greg-nicotera.

Lathem, Laurie. "Breaking Into the Film and TV Industries." business.com. February 22, 2017. https://www.business.com/articles/breaking-into-the-film-and-television-industries.

Sage, Lily. "What I Learned About Life from Being a Makeup Artist." Sage Beauty Blog. June 12, 2017. https://sagebeautyblog.com/2017/06/12/what-i-learned-about-life-from-being-a-makeup-artist.

Tourres, Marie. "How Do You Become a Hairstylist for the TV & Movie Industries?" *Fab Beauty*. July 17, 2017. https://www.fab-beauty.com/on-trend/2017/07/become-hairstylist-movie.

Woodbridge, John. "Tips: Make-Up for HD." BBC. Accessed March 15, 2018. http://www.bbc.co.uk/academy/production/article/art20130702112136285.

INDEX

Page numbers in **boldface**
  are illustrations

ABOUT THE AUTHOR

Jeri Freedman has a bachelor of arts degree from Harvard University. She is the past director of the Boston Playwrights' Lab, an organization that produced original plays in Boston, Massachusetts, and is a published playwright. She is also the author of more than fifty young adult nonfiction books, including *Exploring Theater: Stage Management in the Theater*, *Exploring Theater: Directing in the Theater*, *Getting to Broadway: How* Annie *Made It to the Stage*, and *Getting to Broadway: How* Wicked *Made It to the Stage*.